Signature

HOUSEWARMING
COCKTAILS

Signature
HOUSEWARMING
COCKTAILS

gatekeeper press

Tampa, Florida

Signature Housewarming Cocktails: A New Homeowner's Guide to Celebrations

Published by Gatekeeper Press
7853 Gunn Hwy, Suite 209
Tampa, FL 33626
www.GatekeeperPress.com

The editorial work for this book is entirely the product of the author. Gatekeeper Press did not participate in and is not responsible for any aspect of this element.

Library of Congress Control Number: 2023940637

ISBN (hardcover): 9781662938313

Table of Contents

Move-In Mimosa 3

Your Signature Housewarming Cocktail 5

Birthday Caketail 7

PB & C 9

Sweetheart Tart 11

Lepreconcoction 13

Sweet Peep 15

May Flower Margarita 17

Watermelon Rocks 19

Bottle Rocket 21

Flaming S'moretini 23

Home Harvest 25

Candy Corntini 27

Perky Turkey 29

Snow Globe 31

Move-In Mimosa

Bust down the front door & pop the cork

Glass: **Flute**
Alcohol: **Champagne/Cava/Prosecco**
Mixer: **Orange Juice**
Garnish: **Orange Slice, Burning Sage**

Recipe:

6 Oz. Of your favorite champagne (Chamomile tea for a mocktail version)

Fresh orange juice to taste

Garnish with an orange slice & a smoking sage leaf

Toast on the front porch

Ring the doorbell & sip away

You've leveled up with this major milestone achieved! This is a significant moment in your life, why not make it memorable with some bubbly? Once you pop the cork and let it spray, use the remainder to fill up your special flutes. But hold on, there's more! Add a sprinkle of salt (or toss it over your shoulder), a time-honored practice to ward off negative energy in your abode. Afterward, put a hint of fresh orange in your flute. In the Chinese language, "orange" and "good luck" sound alike, which is why this tradition is ubiquitously observed across the globe. Light some sage for purification and ring the doorbell to announce your arrival. You are finally HOME!!! Now, sit back and savor the moment.

Your Signature Housewarming Cocktail

Raise a glass to homeownership

Glass: Pick a fun glass that speaks to you and the theme
Alcohol: House Choice
Mixer: House Choice
Garnish: House Choice

Your first name(s) + street or community name + punch/
shooter//concoction/libation/aperitif/booze/brew/
refresher/sipper/potion/swigger/toaster/potation/spirit/
quaffer/spritz

Mix and match your most beloved tastes to invent a delicious creation. Keep
in mind the flavorings and trimmings offered within your vicinity, such as local
fruits, garnishes and distilleries. Then call it something creative. Draw inspiration
from your new street, township, or community names…or even your own personal
name. Craft your brand-new drink in a distinct receptacle, then share it with loved
ones as you celebrate your new home. Keep in mind, this is your time to shine.
You've put in the effort to create this fantastic occasion, so whip up a beverage that
perfectly embodies your style.

Birthday Caketail

Double Whammy Jammy

It's your birthday!!! Yeah, it's your birthday!!! Happy birthday to you! Congrats on moving into your new place! Let's get the party started and make this birthday celebration one to remember. Make it as fun as possible and don't forget to wish your new home a happy birthday too. Here's to another year of amazing memories! It's party time!!! Have another one to grow on!

Glass: Stemless wine glass

Alcohol: Cake Vodka, White Chocolate Liqueur, Amaretto

Mixer: Half & Half, Edible Glitter

Garnish: Cotton Candy, Honey, Sprinkles

Recipe:

Rim with honey and rainbow sprinkles

2 parts Cake Vodka

2 parts half & half

1 part white chocolate liqueur

1 part amaretto

Edible blue or pink glitter

Shake with ice and strain into glass

Cotton candy garnish

PB & C

Peanut butter cuptacular cocoa

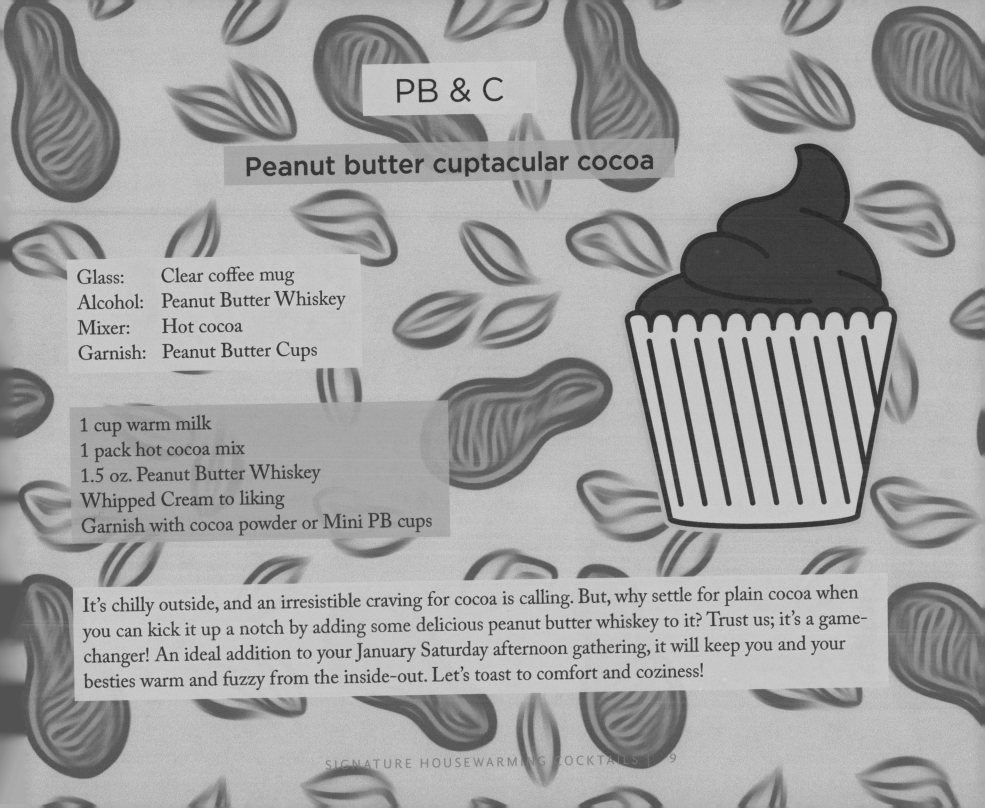

Glass: Clear coffee mug
Alcohol: Peanut Butter Whiskey
Mixer: Hot cocoa
Garnish: Peanut Butter Cups

1 cup warm milk
1 pack hot cocoa mix
1.5 oz. Peanut Butter Whiskey
Whipped Cream to liking
Garnish with cocoa powder or Mini PB cups

It's chilly outside, and an irresistible craving for cocoa is calling. But, why settle for plain cocoa when you can kick it up a notch by adding some delicious peanut butter whiskey to it? Trust us; it's a game-changer! An ideal addition to your January Saturday afternoon gathering, it will keep you and your besties warm and fuzzy from the inside-out. Let's toast to comfort and coziness!

Sweetheart Tart

Everybody get your heart on

Glass: Stemless Coupe Glass
Alcohol: Strawberry Schnapps, Amaretto, Crème de cacao, Bailey's
Mixer: Heavy Cream
Garnish: Strawberries, Candy Hearts

Love is in the atmosphere! It's the perfect time to share this pink potion that is sure to please your picky peeps. Enjoy the juicy sweetness of fresh strawberries and the buzz of a potent cocktail, all while basking in the warm feeling of togetherness. Invite your loved ones to join you in this indulgent and romantic experience.

Recipe:

Rim glass with frosting and heart sprinkles

1 part Strawberry Schnapps

1 part Crème de noyaux or Amaretto

1 part Crème de cacao

1 part Bailey's strawberries & cream

1 part Heavy cream

Sliced strawberries

Shake with ice and strain into glass

Candy hearts garnish

Lepreconcoction

Kiss me or pinch me

Glass:	Cocktail Coupe
Alcohol:	Midori, Vodka, Cointeau
Mixer:	Lemon Juice
Garnish:	Clover or lucky charm

2 parts Midori
1 part Vodka
1 part Cointreau
1 part Lemon juice

Shake with ice and
strain into glass
Garnish with a clover

Are you feeling lucky? It's a grand day for a
housewarming. Invite all you friends to go on the tear at
your place. Don't let your friends get fluttered. And, as they say,
if you're lucky enough to be Irish, you're lucky enough.

Sweet Peep

Hop on in

Glass: **Large Shot glass**
Alcohol: **Blackberry Brandy, Blue Curacao**
Mixer: **Pineapple Juice**
Garnish: **Marshmallow Peep**

Recipe:

1 part Blackberry Brandy

1 part Blue Curaçao

1 part Pineapple Juice

Slow pour each ingredient over spoon & layer

Marshmallow Peep for garnish

Spring has sprung! It's officially the season of blossoms, new life and celebration. The cheerful chickadees are already nesting! Surprise your guests with a festive cocktail that looks just like an Easter egg dye kit. And for those who have recently moved into a new home, take a break and enjoy the deliciously fruity flavors of the season with some jellybeans. So, kick back, relax, and enjoy the beauty of spring!

May Flower Margarita

Flower Power

Glass: Margarita Glass
Alcohol: Tequila, Elderflower Liqueur
Mixer: Lime Juice, Agave or simple syrup
Garnish: Lime wheel, fragrant flower

Salted rim
1 part Tequila
1 part Elderflower Liqueur
1 part Lime Juice
1 part Agave or simple syrup
Shake with ice and strain into glass
Lime wheel & white gardenia flower garnish

April showers brought you flowers. A fabulously refreshing margarita with delicate floral hints feels fresh and springy - an amazing complement to any spring gathering. And if you adorn it with natural treasures from your fresh garden, it's even more spectacular.

Watermelon Rocks

Summertime Splash

Glass: Rocks Glass
Alcohol: Rum, Watermelon liqueur
Mixer: Lime juice, orange juice
Garnish: Green sugar, frozen watermelon cubes

Green sugar rim

Frozen watermelon cubes for ice

1 part Rum

1 part Watermelon liqueur

1 part Lime juice

1/2 part Orange Juice

Shake with ice and strain over watermelon cubes

Can you think of anything more refreshing than chilled watermelon on a scorching summer day? Well, what if it's a spiked watermelon? Let's gather all the summer picnic essentials and have an epic summer smorgasbord smash! Don't forget to freeze your watermelon chunks or balls beforehand.

Bottle Rocket

You're a firework, baby

Glass: Old fashioned milk bottle
Alcohol: Blue raspberry schnapps
Mixer: Grenadine, lemonade
Garnish: Pop rocks, sparklers

1 part Blue raspberry schnapps
1 part Grenadine
2 parts Lemonade
Slow pour each ingredient over spoon & layer
Garnish with Pop rocks & sparklers

Boom, boom, boom! Be the firecracker Jacker with your favorite people at your very first backyard barbecue. Get ready to sizzle and shine at your first backyard barbecue with your favorite folks! Remember to prioritize safety and protect yourself when handling bottle rockets. Once the party starts heating up, who knows what kind of spectacle you'll create for your guests!

Flaming S'moretini

Let's get lit

Glass: Stemless martini glass

Alcohol: Chocolate Liqueur, marshmallow vodka

Mixer: Heavy cream

Garnish: Flaming marshmallow

This drink is fire! Are you ready to burn away the last days of your summer? There is no better way to end the season than a gathering of loved ones in your new backyard around your new firepit toasting one more s'more and being lit one s'more time.

Rim glass with Hershey's syrup

Dip rim in Graham Cracker crumbs

1 part Chocolate liqueur on bottom

1 part Marshmallow vodka shaken with

1 part heavy cream

Slow pour shaken ingredients over spoon & layer

Garnish w/ bamboo skewered marshmallow

Light marshmallow on fire

Home Harvest

Remember September

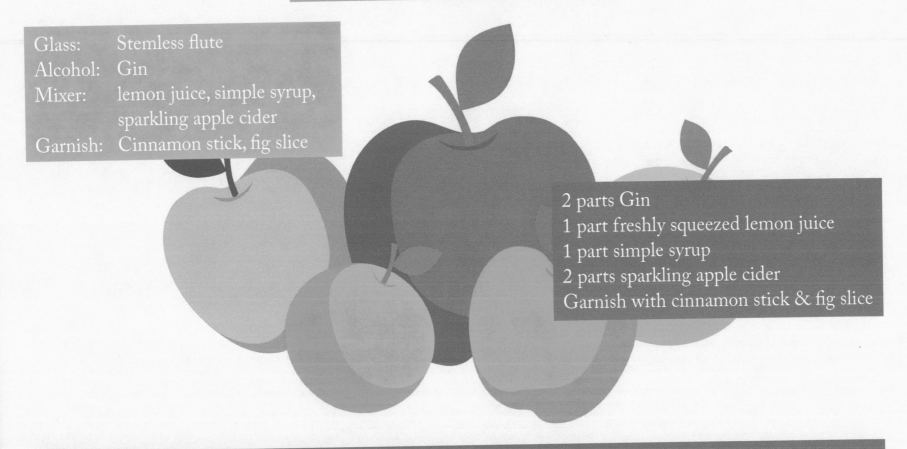

Glass: Stemless flute
Alcohol: Gin
Mixer: lemon juice, simple syrup,
          sparkling apple cider
Garnish: Cinnamon stick, fig slice

2 parts Gin
1 part freshly squeezed lemon juice
1 part simple syrup
2 parts sparkling apple cider
Garnish with cinnamon stick & fig slice

The autumn weather has started chasing away the heat. Leaves have begun their natural transformation while giving us a sight to behold. Nature's slow scenery change & the tree's vibrant costume change brings us to the season's best offerings of cinnamon, pine, apples and bubbles.

Candy Corntini

Trick or Treat

Glass: Martini Glass
Alcohol: Candy corn infused vodka
Mixer: Orange juice
Garnish: Cool whipcream, candy corn

It's an itsy bitsy teeny weeny boozy Halloweeny martini. You could decorate your brand new home like a big haunted house on move in day, or you could just make the candiest and corniest martini of the year. Trick or treat your friends. BOO-YAH!

1 part Candy corn infused vodka (simply pour vodka over a handful of candy corn and let the sugars infuse the vodka for a few hours ahead of time.)

1 part Orange Juice

Slow pour each ingredient over spoon & layer

Cool whipcream smoothed over top

Garnish with Candy Corn

Perky Turkey

Gobble till you wobble

Glass: Cocktail coupe or mason jar
Alcohol: Spiced rum, butterscotch schnapps
Mixer: Apple cider, cranberry juice, lime
Garnish: Apple slice, cranberries or
            pomegranate

So, it seems Tom Turkey escaped his certain fate on a dinner plate. You might say he is feeling pretty perky about it, too. With the full flavors of fall in this quaffer, you might just forget about the rest of the feast. Pour one for yourself, and another for Tom as you both gobble up the fall afternoon!

2 parts Spiced Rum
1 part butterscotch schnapps
1 part Apple Cider
1 part cranberry juice
Splash lime
Garnish with fresh cranberries
Apple slice

Snow Globe

Make it a snow day

Glass: Flute
Alcohol: Champagne, Cava or Prosecco
Mixer: Fruit preserves
Garnish: Sugar, rosemary sprign

Wet entire exterior of glass and roll in sugar

1 part Blackberry/strawberry/blueberry preserves

5 parts Champagne

Garnish carefully with Rosemary sprig

It's that time again! Break out your cozy sweaters, hit the slopes for some skiing, and get ready for snow-filled fun with Santa and snow globes. Let's shake them up. But But not your bubbly...you'll end up with a big mess on your hands & all the elves have their hands too full to come clean it up.. And don't forget to jazz up your cocktails with some festive and fun garnishes. Cheers to the season!

Printed in the USA
CPSIA information can be obtained
at www.ICGtesting.com
LVHW060729291023
762209LV00023B/492